BOYZ II MEN

AFRICAN-AMERICAN ACHIEVERS

BOYZ II MEN

James Earl Hardy

CHELSEA HOUSE PUBLISHERS
Philadelphia

Chelsea House Publishers

Editorial Director   Richard Rennert
Production Manager   Pamela Loos
Art Director   Sara Davis
Picture Editor   Judy Hasday

Staff for BOYZ II MEN

Senior Editors   Philip Koslow/Jane Shumate
Associate Editor   Therese De Angelis
Editorial Assistant   Kristine Brennan
Designer   Takeshi Takahashi
Picture Researcher   Pat Burns

First Printing

1 3 5 7 9 8 6 4 2

Library of Congress Cataloging-in-Publication Data

Hardy, James Earl.
Boyz II Men / James Earl Hardy

    p. cm.—(Black Americans of Achievement)
Includes bibliographical references and index.
Summary: Describes the development of the music group
that was the first to break Elvis Presley's record for length of
time as number one on the pop chart.

ISBN   0-7910-2599-3 (hc.)
ISBN   0-7910-2583-7 (pbk.)

1. Boyz II Men (Musical group)—Juvenile literature. 2.
Rock musicians—United States—Biography—Juvenile lit-
erature. [1. Boyz II Men (Musical group) 2. Musicians. 3.
Afro-Americans—Biography. 4. Rock music.] I. Title.
ML3930.B69H37 1996
782.42'1643'0922—dc20   95-38703
[B]   CIP
                                         AC MN

*Frontis: Boyz II Men in perfor-
mance during the 1995 Grammy
awards show in Los Angeles.
During the evening, Boyz II Men
received awards for Best Album
and Best Performance by an R&B
Duo or Group.*

CONTENTS

AFRICAN-AMERICAN ACHIEVERS

BOYZ II MEN

1

Conquering the King

THERE IS AN old saying that records are made to be broken, but in the music business there was one record everyone expected to stand forever. It was held by the man known as the King, and it seemed unlikely he would ever be dethroned.

A new kind of music called rock and roll was sweeping the nation in the 1950s, and Elvis Presley was its most spectacular figure. His rhythm-and-blues-influenced vocals and high-powered stage performances sent America's teenagers into such frenzies that some politicians, religious leaders, and parents actually believed that he was a disciple of the devil and had possessed the younger generation. But their low opinion of Elvis did not stop sales of his singles and albums from going through the roof; if anything, his image as a dangerous rebel made him even more appealing to the young. He was all over pop radio and ranked high on the record charts published every week by *Billboard* magazine, the bible of the music business. Among Presley's greatest triumphs was a two-sided hit that made history

Even this seemingly casual photo of Boyz II Men—(left to right) Wanya Morris, Nate Morris, Shawn Stockman, and Michael McCary—conveys the romantic, soulful tone of the group's music.

in 1956 when it spent an unprecedented 12 weeks at the number-one spot on the pop chart: the first side of the disk was "Hound Dog" (perhaps the most famous song in the entire Presley repertoire), and the second was "Don't Be Cruel."

For decades, Elvis's record remained untouched; not even the Beatles and the Supremes, the two most popular groups of the 1960s, were able to challenge him. In the following years, two artists did come close. Debby Boone's 1977 version of the easy-listening standard "You Light Up My Life" stayed in the top spot for 10 weeks. Three years later, Olivia Newton-John's "Physical" dominated the charts with a 10-week run. Elvis appeared to be untouchable. But suddenly, in 1992, four young men from Philadelphia, Pennsylvania, conquered the King.

Barely out of their teens, Boyz II Men had just won their first Grammy award for Best Rhythm and Blues (R&B) Vocal Performance by a Duo or Group. The prestigious award followed the tremendous success of their debut album, *Cooleyhighharmony*, which had sold over six million copies. The group's victory was even more significant in light of the other artists nominated in the category: Boyz II Men had beat out established stars such as Aretha Franklin, Luther Vandross, Prince, and Gladys Knight.

Boyz II Men's Grammy victory drew praise from many people in the music industry, but others felt that the Boyz really had not paid their dues. Skeptics pointed out that the young Philadelphians were in a highly competitive arena where an artist is only as good as his or her last hit; they wondered if Boyz II Men would be able to live up to the hype surrounding them. Other young, hip performers had come along before and won a Grammy their first time around, but many of them—such as Christopher Cross, Cyndi Lauper, and Tracy Chapman— had all but faded from public view in a fairly short time. Boyz II Men not only silenced the cynics. They went on to make history.

It all started when they were approached by L. A. Reid and Babyface, two of the hottest talents in music. The songwriting and producing duo had created hits for a long list of artists, including Karyn White, Bobby Brown, New Edition, and Johnny Gill. L. A. and Babyface invited Boyz II Men to perform a composition called "End of the Road," which was slated for the sound track of an upcoming Eddie Murphy film, *Boomerang*. The Boyz had long been fans of L. A. and Babyface, and they jumped at the chance.

Though Boyz II Men's growing popularity was certainly going to be an asset to the project, they were not the real stars of the sound track. *Boomerang*'s music was designed to introduce the moviegoing public to a number of artists featured on L. A. and Babyface's record label, LaFace. Those acts included the female hip-hop soul trio TLC and the vocalist Toni Braxton, whose soul singing, reminiscent of Anita Baker, was showcased on two tracks: "Love Shoulda Brought You Home" and "Give U My Heart," a duet with Babyface that was the sound track's first single.

Thus, when "End of the Road" was released as a single in the summer of 1992, its success took everyone by surprise, including Boyz II Men. They had recorded the song under pressing circumstances: at the time, they were touring as the opening act for Hammer's "Too Legit to Quit" tour, and they only had a few hours to spare between shows. "We lived with the tape [of the song] for a few days [before recording it]," recalls Boyz member Nathan "Nate" Morris. "And we didn't rehearse it at all."

The end result gave no indication of this casual approach. A plush mid-tempo ballad, "End of the Road" is a song with simple but catchy lyrics. The vocals are so polished and passionate that many

Elvis Presley responds to the enthusiasm of teenage fans during an outdoor concert in 1956, when his double-sided single "Hound Dog / Don't Be Cruel" spent a record 12 weeks at the top of the pop music chart. Thirty-six years later, Boyz II Men broke Presley's record when their "End of the Road" remained in the number-one spot for 13 weeks.

Rob Pillatus and Fabrice Morvan, known as Milli Vanilli, receive an American Music award in 1990. The pop music industry was deeply embarrassed the following year when the duo revealed that they had not done the singing on their best-selling album Girl You Know It's True.

critics have compared the Boyz to classic close-harmony groups such as the Temptations. It was only fitting that Boyz II Men and the Tempts were under contract to the same label—Motown Records.

The success of "End of the Road" marked a decisive return of harmony to the realm of pop music. Along with the female quartet En Vogue, Boyz II Men helped bring back good old-fashioned singing, where the voice is employed like a musical instrument and the singer works to produce a beautiful sound as well as to present the lyrics. This was a definite departure from pop music in the 1980s, when synthesized sound and the music video gained more prominence in the industry. While the new techniques helped to sell songs and introduce new groups to the public, many artists were able to score major hits on the pop charts because of the way they looked or danced, not because of their vocal artistry. Whether an artist could actually sing seemed to matter very little; almost anyone's voice could be enhanced by electronic wizardry until it was at least passable. The flashy and sometimes trashy image became more important than anything else.

This style-over-substance formula reached its peak with Milli Vanilli. The dreadlocked duo from Germany—Rob Pillatus and Fabrice Morvan—exploded on the music scene in 1989 with *Girl You Know It's True*, a collection of light dance tracks. While music critics unanimously dismissed Milli Vanilli as soulless and empty (one labeled them "freeze-dried pop"), their videos were MTV favorites. Milli Vanilli (which means "positive energy" in Turkish) danced up a storm while showing off their highly toned physiques, tossing their locks for full effect. They rarely performed in public, and when they did, they always used a prerecorded music track complete with vocals. Thus, Milli Vanilli's videos were solely responsible for the sale of seven million copies of their debut album in the United States.

Having preteens clawing at them and collecting a slew of American Music awards (which are given out for popularity, not musical excellence) was one thing. But when Milli Vanilli received a Grammy for Best New Artist, the award was greeted with surprise and displeasure by many people in the music industry. A number of insiders suspected that Pillatus and Morvan had not actually done much, if any, singing on their album; thus, they did not deserve to be called artists at all, let alone the best new artists of the year.

Milli Vanilli and their producer, Frank Farian, knew that the rumors were true, but so far no one had been able to prove anything. Morvan and Pillatus felt that they could save the situation and answer their critics by doing the vocals on their second album. Farian clearly felt that they were not good enough to bring it off; he refused, and they fired him. Farian retaliated by publicly confirming the rumors that had been floating around for months: Milli Vanilli had not sung a single note on their debut album.

Pillatus and Morvan now had to face the music. They immediately called a press conference; while admitting they had deceived the public, they said they had "made a pact with the devil" in order to achieve fame and fortune. "We were living together in the projects in Munich, we had nothing to eat, and we wanted to be stars," explained Pillatus as Morvan looked on. "And suddenly, this guy [Farian] gave us a chance and we took it." The press coaxed them into singing live, to show the world that they could do it if they had to—but their efforts proved that Farian had been right. As *Time* magazine observed, "Their performance proved that looking good was what they did best." The National Academy of Recording Arts and Sciences, the organization that awards the Grammys, agreed: embarrassed by the hoax, they stripped Milli Vanilli of their Best New Artist award.

The "Is it live or is it Memorex?" controversy did not end with Milli Vanilli, though. One of the acts vying for the Best New Artist Grammy against Boyz II Men in 1992 was C & C Music Factory. C & C also had to ward off charges of fraud. The controversy began when a veteran session singer, Martha Wash, accused the group of using her vocals on the song "Gonna Make You Sweat," a number-one pop smash, but allowing someone else to lip-sync them in the video.

No one suggested that Boyz II Men had any similar problem. But some observers believed that the academy, frightened of another Milli Vanilli scandal, decided to steer clear of both groups. They passed over Boyz II Men and C & C Music Factory and gave the award to vocalist-guitarist Marc Cohn. Cohn's folk-pop sound was squarely in the middle of the road, reminding many listeners of the work of Carly Simon, James Taylor, and Carole King.

But when "End of the Road" was released, everyone understood that Boyz II Men was the genuine article. The record became the group's first number-one pop single. Moreover, "End of the Road" stayed at the top of the charts for a total of 13 weeks, eclipsing Elvis Presley's seemingly unbreakable mark.

Many found it hard to believe that a posse of young men only a couple of years out of high school could suddenly take Elvis's title. But there was now no question that Boyz II Men had captured the hearts of millions worldwide, and the music industry got the message. Within a year, almost a dozen other male vocal groups came on the scene, trying to duplicate the success of the Boyz. Unfortunately, none of them could come close. Boyz II Men, with their clean-cut image and teenybopping hip-hop pop sound, were unique.

Though their record-breaking hit was about the end of a love affair, "End of the Road" really signaled the beginning of a musical legend. Like many great sagas in the history of American music, the story of Boyz II Men is one of talent, dedication, hard work, and faith winning out over forces that have blighted the lives of countless young people.

Accompanied by their manager and producer, Michael Bivins (center), Boyz II Men celebrate their 1992 Grammy award for Best Vocal Performance by an R&B Duo or Group.

2

Boyz from the Hood

THE BOYZ OF Boyz II Men—Mike McCary, Nathan Morris, Wanya Morris, and Shawn Stockman—all were born within two years of each other in Philadelphia, Pennsylvania. Their native city boasted an illustrious legacy of freedom and tolerance, but its black citizens had often found it a difficult—and sometimes hostile—environment.

African Americans have been an important presence in Philadelphia since its founding in 1682, a century before the United States came into being. The city's founder was William Penn, an Englishman who believed passionately in religious freedom. Penn, the son of a high-ranking admiral in the British navy, was a member of the Society of Friends, also known as the Quakers, a group that had broken away from the established Church of England. The Quakers' ideas about religion brought them into conflict with the authorities, and Penn

A 19th-century engraving of the Friends Meeting House on Cherry Street in Philadelphia. Commonly known as Quakers, members of the Society of Friends played a leading role in founding the city during the 17th century; because of the Quakers' belief in religious and racial tolerance, Philadelphia became known as the City of Brotherly Love.

was thrown into jail a number of times for spreading Quaker teachings.

In those days, one way of getting rid of troublesome characters was to send them to Britain's colonies in the Americas. Thus, in 1681, Penn received a charter from the British king, Charles II, to found a new settlement to the west of the established colonies of New York and Massachusetts Bay. The new territory came to be called Pennsylvania. The colony's capital, established the following year at the meeting point of two great rivers, later known as the Schuylkill and the Delaware, was called Philadelphia, combining two Greek words to mean "brotherly love."

From the beginning, Penn and his followers strove to make their colony live up to the name of its capital, as a haven where all people would be treated equally and fairly. They did not follow other European newcomers who forcibly displaced the numerous Native American tribes who had occupied the land for many centuries; instead, the Quakers treated the Indians like brethren and sought to live side by side with them in harmony, sharing the land. The Quakers also condemned the enslavement of Africans, who were then being brought to the colonies by the thousands and put to work for white masters. Accordingly, Pennsylvania tried to discourage slaving by charging slave merchants a high tax for every African imported into the state, and by 1750 the traffic in slaves virtually ceased. At the same time the city became a haven for slaves who won their freedom or escaped from bondage. By 1780, when Pennsylvania outlawed slavery completely, Philadelphia had a black population of more than 6,000.

It was only fitting that Philadelphia should become the cradle of the American Revolution. The Declaration of Independence, asserting the rights of American citizens and severing the bond

Richard Allen (1760-1831) was the first great black leader in U.S. history. Born as a slave in Philadelphia, Allen purchased his freedom, obtained an education, and became a minister. As the founder of the African Methodist Episcopal church, he inspired African Americans to fight for freedom and equality.

between the 13 colonies and Great Britain, was signed in Philadelphia's Independence Hall in 1776. After the triumph of the revolution, Philadelphia was again the center of historic events, as the new nation's leaders met in Independence Hall to draft the Constitution of the United States in 1787. Following the creation of the new nation, Philadelphia served as the capital of the United States between 1790 and 1800.

As these events unfolded, no individual exemplified the black experience in Philadelphia better than Richard Allen. Born as a slave in the city in 1760, Allen eventually purchased his freedom and became a preacher in the Methodist church. A brilliant organizer and speaker, Allen inspired blacks to fight for their rights as American citizens. He founded the African Methodist Episcopal church, the nation's first great black religious organization, and led it until his death in 1831. In future generations, such outstanding black leaders as Frederick Douglass and the Reverend Martin Luther King, Jr., were to advance the principles expressed by Allen at the time of the nation's founding.

Despite Philadelphia's early legacy of freedom, the city did not always remain a haven for African Americans. As white European immigrants began to settle in Philadelphia during the 19th century, raising the city's population toward the one million mark, discrimination and occasional violence against the city's 40,000 blacks were all too common. Whenever the nation's economy took a downturn and hard times descended on the city, Philadelphia's blacks always bore the greatest burden.

The fortunes of Philadelphia's African Americans did not really improve until the mid–20th century, when political reformers cleaned up the city's government and opened municipal jobs to blacks. By 1963, African Americans held more than 11,000 of the 28,000 city jobs and made up about 30 percent of teachers in the public schools. However, living conditions in areas such as North and South Philadelphia improved very slowly, and the frustration of black residents erupted in riots during 1963 and 1964.

Both the federal government and the city administration made some effort to alleviate social problems with antipoverty funds, but the money was inadequate to combat the tide of poverty, crime, and drugs afflicting some inner-city neighborhoods. Motivated by fears of racial unrest, Philadelphians in 1971 elected Frank Rizzo, a former police commissioner with a law-and-order approach, as their mayor. During Rizzo's two terms, discontent within the black community was widespread, and the division between black and white Philadelphians appeared to widen.

Philadelphia enjoyed a new beginning when the city's first black mayor, W. Wilson Goode, took office in 1983. The son of a North Carolina sharecropper, Goode had worked his way through college and migrated to Philadelphia, where he distinguished himself as a public housing official and then served as the city's managing director, second in command to the mayor. Finally, after defeating Rizzo in the Democratic party primary, he won a three-way election and began his tenure in Philadelphia's historic City Hall.

Goode had the misfortune to take office at a time when the nation's economy was in turmoil and the federal government, under President Ronald Reagan, was cutting back on aid to the nation's cities and sabotaging efforts to secure the civil rights of black Americans and other minority groups. Moreover, whatever progress Goode's administration made was finally undermined by the terrible events that unfolded in West Philadelphia in May 1985.

Members of the Philadelphia group MOVE, which advocated a natural way of life, racial justice, and armed resistance to authority. In the eyes of MOVE and many other Philadelphians, the city's proud history as a haven for African Americans was only a distant memory.

The trouble arose from a conflict between the Philadelphia police and MOVE, a predominantly black group that espoused a number of causes, including protection for the environment and racial justice. But they were also heavily armed and had had several clashes with the police over the years. Finally, on May 13, the police moved against them in force, determined to evict MOVE from their row house at 6221 Osage Avenue, in a low-income, racially mixed neighborhood. Some members of the group responded with a hail of gunfire, much of it coming from a fortified bunker on the roof of the house.

The police believed that if they could knock out the bunker, they would be able to enter the house without suffering major casualties. They decided to blow the bunker apart with a carefully constructed bomb dropped from a helicopter. Unfortunately, the bomb ignited a can of gasoline, and the roof of the house began to burn. Firefighters were on the scene, but half an hour went by before they were sent into action. By that time, the upper floor of the MOVE house was a mass of flames, and the fire began spreading to neighboring houses. Before the fire-fighters could bring the blaze under control, it had engulfed everything in its path. On May 14, the 6200 block of Osage Avenue and two adjacent streets looked like a war zone. Sixty-one houses had been destroyed, and 250 people had lost their homes and all of their belongings. Worse still, 11 charred bodies were found inside the rubble of the MOVE house—and 5 of the dead were children.

In the wake of the tragedy, the police commissioner and the managing director resigned, and Mayor Goode appointed a commission to investigate the disaster. The commission's report blamed the mayor himself and numerous other officials for a host of misjudgments and tactical errors, not the least of them being the decision to drop a bomb on

a house in a densely populated area. Because of his willingness to accept blame for the disaster, Mayor Goode managed to win reelection in 1988 by a narrow margin, and the city administration subsequently rebuilt the burned-out homes. However, Goode's once-bright future in politics was blighted forever; the national image of Philadelphia was tarnished; and Philadelphians' faith in the future was deeply shaken. Just six months after the MOVE tragedy, in fact, Goode had to declare a state of emergency in a neighborhood where angry whites were marching in the streets, trying to force a number of black families from their newly purchased homes. In this difficult atmosphere, the young men who became Boyz II Men had to deal with not only the usual challenges of adolescence but also a variety of complex family situations.

Michael "Mike" McCary was born on December 16, 1971, in North Philadelphia. McCary, though,

An aerial view of the devastation wrought by the Osage Avenue fire on May 13, 1985, when Philadelphia police bombed a house occupied by MOVE. Though city authorities later rebuilt the burned-out homes, the MOVE tragedy dealt a severe blow to Philadelphia's image and civic pride.

Michael McCary was one of six children raised by a single parent in North Philadelphia. He recalled that his mother, Omarnetta Thomas, "did everything possible to make [the family] feel happy and secure."

is not his original family name. His father was born Albert Williams but later changed his name to Robert Lewis McCary because he was often in trouble with the law. His son Michael described him as "a man of different traits who never held a steady legal job." Pursuing this irregular lifestyle, Robert Lewis McCary spent little time with his family, and he died before Michael could even learn much about him. Michael's mother, Omarnetta Thomas, worked as a nurse in order to support him and his five siblings (four brothers and a sister). As a result, Michael remembered, the McCarys "were always struggling to make ends meet. This made it difficult to be relaxed but my mom did everything possible to make us feel happy and secure."

Nathan "Nate" Morris, born in South Philadelphia on June 18, 1971, had an even harder time than Mike. His father left home around the time of Nate's birth. Though his mother, Gail Harris, worked in a local bank, she earned a small salary and found it nearly impossible to support her four children alone. (Nate has two sisters and a brother.) As Nate later said, "We went without gas, electric, water and a phone at different times. Sometimes we were so hungry that we had to borrow food from people who lived in our neighborhood. Kids at school teased and harassed me about these things. They said horrendous things about my mom not being able to afford the bare necessities in life. I used to get beat up so much in school over it that it wasn't funny." Looking back on those days after becoming a successful performer, he realized that attending church, sometimes almost seven days a week, kept him centered and sane. "It was our faith that brought us through those hard times," he said.

Wanya (pronounced WAN-yay) Morris was born in North Philadelphia on July 29, 1973. Though he is not related to Nate Morris, he grew up under similar conditions. His parents, Carla Morris and Dallas Thornton, broke up when he was a toddler. As a result, Wanya's family (which, like Nate's, includes a brother and two sisters) had to go on welfare. During his early years, the family lived in the Richard Allen projects and then moved to a depressed neighborhood known as Germantown. At the time, Wanya had little hope for a better life beyond his surroundings. "The projects were basically supposed to be a stepping stone," he told the author Rita Henderson. "People were expected to stay there for a brief period of time until they got back on their feet. To me, it seemed like we were always going to stay there. I never saw our progres-

When Nathan "Nate" Morris was growing up in South Philadelphia, his family often found it hard to afford the bare necessities of life. "It was our faith that brought us through those hard times," he later said.

sion toward that step up to a better place. Things were just bad for a very long time."

To make matters worse, his mother's boyfriend, the father of his younger siblings, physically abused Wanya. "I don't know why he didn't like me, but I do know that he used to beat the crap out of me for no reason," Wanya later recalled. The beatings stopped only when his mother ended her relationship with the man.

Shawn Stockman, born in Southwest Philadelphia on September 26, 1972, later said, "I had a very good childhood despite the typical things that a black kid living in the ghetto goes through."

According to Shawn, the credit for that belongs to his mother, JoAnn: "She was really good at shielding things from us, like not having enough money. She held down a couple of jobs and wouldn't get a lot of things for herself so that her five kids could always have all of the necessities. And, even though we didn't have gas or electric a lot of times, she didn't get upset about that in front of us or make that an issue. She always kept her worries to herself. And, because she was so strong, we were, too."

In addition to the economic hardships they faced, the young men had to deal with their peers. "I tended to get laughed at in school because I was in the honor roll society and on the debate team," Mike recalled. Shawn, always shy, loved to read, and that pastime did not sit well with some of his rougher schoolmates. Nate was also shy, but he was not inclined to let anybody take advantage of him. "Most of the time, I was quiet until people started messing with me," he revealed. "I was one of those kids that, if someone hit me, I would get them back."

Despite the hardships, life was not all bleak. Nate fondly remembers playing baseball with a whiffle bat and a tennis ball every day after school and going fishing with his brother, Alphonso. He also took part in pranks, such as hopping freight trains. "Back then, it was fun," he admitted. "But it was also dangerous. Now that I'm an adult, I don't condone kids doing it."

Shawn recalled that he and his brothers and sisters always found ways of amusing themselves. "Every Sunday was a special sports day," he told Rita Henderson. "We planned our activities around whatever sport was being televised. If it was football night, we got out our little Nerf football. If basketball came on, we would make a basketball out of aluminum foil. For a basket, we would bend a hanger into the shape of a half circle, and hang it on the

As a youngster in the inner city, moving from one depressed neighborhood to another, Wanya Morris had little hope for a better life: "It seemed like we were always going to stay [in the projects]."

lintel of both sides of the doorway. We could then play basketball on full court, while watching the game." But with so many people dribbling, throwing, catching, and dunking, accidents were bound to happen: "Sometimes we would end up wrecking our mom's furniture while jumping all over the place. She'd get upset but knew we were just trying to enjoy ourselves."

There was one thing Shawn, Mike, Nate, and Wanya had in common while they were growing up—they all sang. In fact, Wanya was virtually born singing. His mother remembered that only a few weeks after his birth, she would be singing a song around the house and Wanya would mimic the sounds in his own way. He might have inherited this ability from his father, who had sung in a gospel group. "It was just etched in [my] soul to love music," he said.

By the time he reached school age, little Wanya was entering and winning local talent shows, singing a cappella versions (without musical accompaniment) of Stevie Wonder songs and of "The Greatest Love of All," one of his all-time favorites, which later became one of Whitney Houston's signature tunes. Because he was always willing to perform, he was sometimes accused of being a ham who craved the spotlight. But the criticism did not bother him: all that mattered were the visions of stardom in his eyes. He also had a talent for drawing, and he believed that he could become a great artist as well as a great singer.

Shawn, for his part, did not initially see music as his ticket out of the hood. He was more interested in an acting career. But his vision of the future changed when he was driving home one day with his mother from one of his acting classes. "[A] song [was] playing on the radio by Jeffrey Osborne called 'On the Wings of Love,'" he recalled. "I started singing it out loud and got hyped with emotion as I went along. As I continued to sing, she stopped the car in the middle of the street. She asked me, 'How did you do that?' I responded, 'How did I do what?' Singing came so natural to me, so I couldn't understand why she was so surprised. She had heard me sing before. But, I don't know, after that day, she just pushed me into music more and more."

Both Shawn's mother and father encouraged him to pursue his dream wisely: "They always told me, 'Whatever career you choose, be the best at it.' But they were concerned because the music industry is volatile. A lot of people don't make it. They told me to put my energies in other places too, just

Like Mike McCary, Shawn Stockman credits his mother for helping him and his four siblings cope with the ordeal of poverty. "[B]ecause she was so strong, we were, too," he recalled.

in case my plan to be a singer . . . didn't work out." His parents were so concerned that he expand his interests that after Boyz II Men was formed, they tried to dissuade him from going to rehearsals, fearing that he was devoting too much time to just one thing.

Both Shawn and Wanya's parents wanted them to attend college, but neither young man was interested. As Wanya recalled, he took his cue from Eddie Murphy: "I was watching TV one night and he told an interviewer he didn't go to college because people used to always say that he needed something to fall back on. When people would say that, it made him feel as though he was setting himself up for failure. Since entertainment was something he wanted to do for the rest of his life, he didn't want to think about failure. That meant a lot to me, and I agree with his reasoning."

But when it came to choosing a high school, all four young men and their parents agreed on one institution. The choice would change their lives forever.

3

High School Harmony

FOR WANYA, ATTENDING the Philadelphia High School of the Creative and Performing Arts— a magnet school that attracted students from a variety of backgrounds—was a dream come true.

"After I saw *Fame*, I knew [it] was the type of school I had to go to," he explained, referring to the 1980 film that chronicled the lives of a group of teens at New York's High School of the Performing Arts. The movie spawned a television series and advanced the careers of actress-director-choreographer Debbie Allen, actress-songwriter Irene Cara, and actor-dancer Michael DeLorenzo.

Wanya's expectations of what he would find at his new school were confirmed on his first day. "Everybody was singing and happy to be back [after summer vacation]," he remembered. "You'd never see that in other schools! It was also a small school, so everybody seemed to know each other. It was very much like a family atmosphere."

In this scene from the 1975 film Fame, *students at New York's High School of the Performing Arts stage a dance number on the streets of Manhattan. After seeing the high-spirited film, Wanya Morris was determined to attend Philadelphia's own performing arts school.*

Certainly, there were adjustments to be made. "Coming from the neighborhoods we were from, we weren't used to hearing a lot of classical music and jazz and opera," Wanya recalled. "So when we got in and heard people singing classical, it was like, 'This ain't what I saw [in the movie and on TV]!' But when you get into it, you realize there are similarities between everything. Knowing all that just makes you a well-rounded musician."

The young men learned that there were benefits to mastering new disciplines. As Mike put it, "With classical as your roots, you can sing just about anything." Classical choral singing—all the Boyz had sung in church choirs—was also a valuable experience. Under the guidance of the school's choral teacher, David King, the young men learned how to use their voices as instruments that would blend together to produce a new sound, just as the strings, brasses, and woodwinds blend together in a symphony orchestra.

Shawn, Mike, Wanya, and Nate soon came to know each other by sight—the school had only 600 students—but each of them had his own running buddies. As Shawn reflected, "It was almost fate that brought us together, four brothers from different sections of the city."

Actually, Boyz II Men began as a quintet. When Nate began forming the group in 1988, his childhood friend Marc Nelson was the first person he turned to. Nate next recruited Wanya, who was the solo king in the school choir; his performance of Michael Jackson's "Man in the Mirror" was a real crowd pleaser. Nate then tapped Shawn. Because his head was always buried in a book, no one had noticed him before—until he got up one day at choral practice and did a solo himself.

Mike, the final member, entered the picture in a very unlikely setting—the bathroom. As Nate explained, "We were in the bathroom singing a song called 'Can You Stand the Rain' by New Edition. We liked [singing in the bathroom] because the acoustics were great. Mike was there, and just added a bass part to the song, and it sounded good. When he asked to join the group, we made him follow us around and keep singing that note until he grew on us."

With this highly informal beginning, Boyz II Men was actually following a long and honorable tradition that dated back to the 1950s, when a new sound emerged to rival the sentimental ballads ("Love Is a Many-Splendored Thing") and inane novelty songs ("How Much Is That Doggy in the Window?") that dominated the charts. It evolved in urban neighborhoods throughout the nation, where young men hung out with their friends on stoops and street corners, in the park, and at the local candy store, crooning and cooing in perfect harmony. In addition to the popular ballads and dance tunes carried by the radio, city neighborhoods were imbued with gospel music from the churches, country blues drifting up from the South, and the innovative sounds being played in jazz clubs. Out of this cultural mix, both rhythm and blues (R&B) and rock and roll were born. When a New York disc jockey named Alan Freed began to play the new sounds on WINS radio during the early 1950s, a revolution in American popular music was under way.

The early groups who blazed a trail in the style of R&B singing that came to be known as doo-wop (from the distinctive sound laid down by the bass singer) began as humbly as Boyz II Men. One day in 1954, for example, Jimmy Keyes and some friends were sitting in a convertible parked on a street in the Bronx, New York. While improvising and harmonizing, Keyes wrote down the basics of a song called "Sh-Boom." Recorded by Keyes's six-member group, the Chords, "Sh-Boom" became the first

The Cadillacs, best known for their 1955 hit single "Speedo," were one of the many successful singing groups to emerge from America's urban neighborhoods during the 1950s and 1960s.

R&B record to crack the top 10. After that, the doo-wop hits came in a flood, as the Bronx alone produced a host of stellar groups that included the Cadillacs, the Harptones, the Tokens, the Wrens, and the Chantels.

Boyz II Men, during their early high school years, did not actually see themselves as a genuine group. They did not even have a name for their ensemble. But it was obvious to those around them that they were serious about singing together. "I would ride them to death because they'd be late to class because they were harmonizing in the halls, but there was never an attitude from any of them," said their principal, Ellen Savitz. "I used to have to kick them out of the auditorium in the late afternoon because they'd always be rehearsing. You just knew they were going to make it; they had all of the confidence that was needed."

The girls in the school noticed, too. "We did not have a lot of money and we're not the most attractive bunch of guys," admitted Wanya. "So, if you could sing, you could get a girl to pay you some attention."

Their arrival as a group became official, though, when the five talented young men made their debut at a Valentine's Day school showcase. Calling themselves Boys to Men (which was the title of another New Edition tune), they did "Can You Stand the Rain" a cappella in the style of Take Six, the gospel-jazz sextet they patterned themselves after. "We've always listened to them," said Shawn about Take Six. "Their blend was so good that we'd sing their songs and always rewind the tape trying to pick out the harmonies."

Even though she knew every one of her students was uniquely talented, Principal Savitz was astounded by the performance. "It was a very magical moment," she recalled. "That was the first time they had done it in a public forum and suddenly all of us realized we were hearing something very special."

The group got a standing ovation from the students and faculty, and the praise caught them by surprise. "We did not expect to get that type of response," Mike admitted. "The other students had heard us numerous times—like in the lunchroom or on the roof—but they said it was like a whole different group up there. And a lot of the girls said they were melting, just falling out of their seats as if it were an actual concert."

At that point, however, the harmony the quintet experienced onstage eluded them everywhere else. Only Nate and Marc were actually close. "We were all vocal majors, and the music was the only thing we had in common," observed Nate. "We had many heated arguments, almost on a daily basis. If it was not about music, it was about girls or some other trivial crap."

Take Six, a highly successful gospel-jazz sextet, had a powerful influence on the young singers who became Boyz II Men. Like Take Six, Boyz II Men would build their appeal on a blend of diverse musical styles and the use of tight harmonies.

Marc's attitude had a great deal to do with this tension. He seemed to instigate most of the disagreements, and he would often pick on Shawn, who was the quietest member of the group. As Shawn later explained, "I did not get along with him because he considered me a nerd. At first I thought everything was cool between us, but then he started talking about me behind my back and doing a lot of little stuff to annoy me." Marc tried hard to get Wanya on his side, and this brought him into conflict with Mike. As Marc's friend, Nate found himself in a difficult position. "I was in between Marc and everyone else in the group, trying to be the arbitrator," Nate recalled, "but my efforts did not work. I was not as outspoken then as I am now, so a lot of things happened that should not have."

Marc also pulled rank on the others to make himself the center of attention. As Nate explained,

> Marc was the kind of person who kind of felt that the universe revolved around him. For example, after our first amateur show at a place called Club Impulse, he asked us to sit on the side for a few minutes. He then whipped out a Bobby Brown album and put on 'My Prerogative' and started singing and dancing along with it [like he was] a solo artist. Things like that went on all the time . . . even when we would pray together. Shawn, Mike, Wan and I would pray for a successful group. Marc would stand there praying for his own individual aspirations.

It became increasingly obvious that Marc wanted to do his own thing, but when he decided to step out and do just that, Nate was stunned and saddened. "When Marc sprung his bad news on us with no notice, the group almost broke up," he said. "We all sat out on my steps, feeling very depressed. When we had five parts, our harmony was tight and our sound was simply incredible. It was like we were the unit, so when he left, it felt like the unit was not whole anymore. Also, for a couple of weeks, it was especially hard for me to adjust. Losing Marc meant more to me than to anyone else because Marc and I were best friends."

But Nate realized that the show had to go on—particularly after Shawn and Wanya made it clear that unless Nate accepted Marc's departure and got on with the business at hand, they could do without him, too. As Nate later reflected, "Marc's departure from the group was for the best anyway. Like anything God plans, things happen for a reason. Even if we had remained as a group, he might have left later on in our career. This news might have been worse then, because we would have debuted as a quintet and then suddenly, we're a quartet. This kind of activity would have made Boyz II Men appear unstable."

As Nate and Mike were getting ready to graduate from high school, the group itself graduated to performing on street corners and subway platforms, at parties, funerals, and talent contests, earning a little pocket change and a host of fans. They knew, though, that local attention was not enough. They had to catch the eye of someone who could open that door to the career they longed for. That opportunity finally arrived when a former member of one of their favorite groups came to town.

4

The New Edition

IN MARCH 1989, the four aspiring singers attended a concert called Power House II, sponsored by radio station Power 99FM, at Philadelphia's Civic Center. The concert was hosted by Bell Biv DeVoe, the vocal trio that had formerly been part of New Edition: Ricky Bell, Michael Bivins, and Ronnie DeVoe. Though they loved Bell Biv DeVoe's music, the Boyz had not come just to catch the performance. As Mike put it, "We wanted the group to hear us sing and maybe get us a record deal."

There was one hitch, however—the Boyz did not have a backstage pass. But they found a way around that obstacle. They hung around the stage door until they managed to get hold of a single pass. The first one in managed to slip the pass back out to his mates, and they repeated the process until they were all inside. As luck would have it, Michael Bivins happened to be coming offstage at the moment they reassembled, and they descended on him.

As Shawn remembered it, the Boyz asked Bivins if they could sing for him. Not surprisingly, Bivins was shocked by their boldness: "He asked, 'You want to do it right here?' And we said, 'Sure.'" Then, in front of an audience that included an all-star lineup

Boyz II Men in Montego Bay, Jamaica, where they performed in December 1990. Though two of the Boyz were still high school students at the time, they already had a record contract and were working hard at polishing their stage technique.

that was sharing the bill with BBD—Paula Abdul, Keith Sweat, Kid-N-Play, Cherrelle, and Will Smith (a.k.a. the Fresh Prince)—the Boyz did a song they knew Bivins would recognize: New Edition's "Can You Stand the Rain." Everyone was impressed, including Bivins, who gave the Boyz his business card.

No doubt because of his busy schedule, Bivins never seemed to be around when Nate called him. But after two months of persistent effort, the Boyz got Bivins to sit down with them at Sylvia's, a celebrated soul-food restaurant in New York's Harlem. During the course of the meal Bivins agreed to become the group's manager, signing them to his company, Biv Entertainment.

It would be a full two years, though, before Boyz II Men's debut album was released. The Boyz had a lot of work to do. Besides working on their style and sound with Bivins and getting a record contract, they were still students. Their parents all insisted that they not jump into a career without first getting their high school diplomas.

Both Nate and Mike graduated in 1990. Shawn would follow them a year later, and so would Wanya—but his degree would not be from Performing Arts. Because he missed his absent friends and was excited about the direction the group was headed in, Wanya started to play around too much in school and found himself expelled. "By the time I found out I should have been doing my homework, my grades were so bad that it was too late for me to even care," he said. "Also, I had learned a lot about music [at Performing Arts], so I really did not feel that there was anything left for me to learn about at the school." He finished his studies at William Penn High and at Willingboro High School in Willingboro, New Jersey, just across the Delaware. "It did not matter to me that it took an additional year for me to graduate," he observed. "The important thing was that I did not quit."

Before all the Boyz had their diplomas, they had a record contract. Recognizing the young group's talent and their potential, Motown Records signed the quartet in 1990.

Motown's own success story—as a company owned and operated by African Americans—was as dramatic in its way as the saga of any singing group. Before Motown's arrival, African-American artists had generally been exploited by the music industry. They received rock-bottom fees for making recordings, and they were often shunted aside in favor of white artists. Such was the case with blues legend Willie Mae "Big Mama" Thornton, who recorded the song "Hound Dog" in 1953 for Peacock, a small Houston-based label. Impressed by Thornton's recording, the giant record company RCA Victor signed Elvis Presley to do a cover version of the song. With Victor's influence and promotional power behind it, Presley's "Hound Dog" became a massive hit with white audiences; Thornton received nothing for her role in developing the music.

The second-class status accorded to black artists began to change in the late 1950s when Berry Gordy, Jr., founded Tamla Records in Detroit. The son of a prosperous businessman, the adventurous Gordy had followed his own path since dropping out of high school: after trying his hand at professional boxing, he had done a stint in the army, operated a record store, and worked as a machinist on the Ford assembly line. But Gordy's true vocation was music; he wrote numerous songs and spent all his free time in various Detroit clubs, meeting musicians and trying to interest them in his material. Gordy's talent and perseverance finally brought success as a number of his tunes became hit recordings: "Lonely Teardrops" and "To Be Loved" by Jackie Wilson; "Money" by Barrett Strong; and "You Got What It Takes" by Marv Johnson.

Michael Bivins agreed to manage Mike, Nate, Wanya, and Shawn in 1989 after they cornered him backstage at a concert and sang for him. He named the quartet Boyz II Men after a hit song recorded by his first singing group, New Edition.

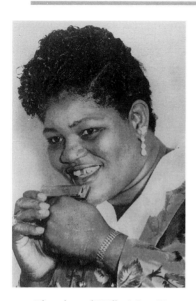

Blues legend Willie Mae "Big Mama" Thornton was one of many African-American musicians who were exploited by the music industry during the 1950s. Thornton made the original recording of "Hound Dog" in 1953, but when Elvis Presley did a smash-hit cover version of the record three years later, Thornton came away empty-handed.

Gordy also delved into record producing, with equally good results. But he knew that he could not depend on established record labels to deliver royalty payments and give his artists the attention they deserved. He also believed that existing record companies were not responding to the tastes of the large black populations in cities such as Detroit. Gordy was convinced that he could build a successful business by offering people high-quality music that spoke to their everyday struggles and aspirations. "Everybody was writing love songs," he later wrote. "I was basically a dreamer of love songs, and that's what I wanted to write, too. But wanting to write love songs and also living in the real world and listening to the earthy problems of life, I tried to mix that up with the love and the feeling."

In addition to his feel for the pulse of the community, Gordy was also a skilled businessman and had a knack for spotting talent. Tamla's headquarters, a small frame house on Detroit's West Grand Boulevard, soon became a center of the city's musical life, attracting a close-knit group of songwriters, singers, and musicians. By 1959, Gordy had his first hit record, "Shop Around" by Smokey Robinson and the Miracles, and Tamla's modest white house was soon known as Hitsville, USA.

In 1962, Gordy renamed his company Motown (after "motor town," a popular nickname for Detroit), and before long the so-called Motown sound was a fixture on the pop culture scene: Gordy's brand of R&B was funky enough for black audiences but also palatable to the white pop radio audience. The Motown recordings merged gospel-infused vocals with over-the-top orchestrations—howling horns, the exciting echo of cymbals and chimes, hip-shaking tambourines, snappy snare drums and congas, and rousing handclaps. Live and vibrant, the Motown sound is so distinctive that even the most casual pop music listener can identify it immediately.

Gordy combined this distinct musical sound with a painstaking attention to style. Under the boss's watchful eye, each performer was molded to carry himself or herself in a way that suggested class and elegance. They were all given tips on how to walk, how to stand, how to go up or down a flight of stairs, how to shake hands and make small talk with reporters, how to bow and curtsy onstage. In Gordy's view, there was no room in the Motown universe for drugs, alcohol, or "hanky-panky," especially when the company's artists were on the road. By presenting his groups as high-class acts, Gordy aimed to get them into arenas that black artists did not normally perform in.

Having found a musical and stylistic groove, Gordy and his associates generated a tidal wave of hit records by artists who soon became legends in the music world: in addition to Smokey Robinson and the Miracles, Motown's roster included the Temptations, the Four Tops, Marvin Gaye, Junior Walker, Mary Wells, Stevie Wonder, the Marvelettes, Martha and the Vandellas, and the Supremes. Over a 10-year period, Motown produced 79 records that ranked in *Billboard*'s top 10, an achievement matched by no other company. Gordy also encouraged and nurtured many up-and-coming songwriters, such as Nick Ashford and Valerie Simpson, Norman Whitfield, and the team of Eddie and Brian Holland and Lamont Dozier.

Spearheaded by the spectacular crossover success of the Supremes, Motown soon emerged as a multimillion-dollar entertainment giant, promoting tours and producing films as well. While it was raking in the profits, Motown remained true to its roots; the company's executives were all black (a number were Gordy's relatives), and artists were treated as members of an extended family, sharing fairly in Motown's lavish success.

The position of black artists in the music world changed dramatically when Berry Gordy founded Tamla Records—later renamed Motown—in 1958. Gordy promoted music reflecting the experience of African Americans, and he ensured that Tamla's performers shared fully in the success of the company.

But by the late 1980s, Motown had relocated to Los Angeles, Gordy had sold his controlling share, and the company had lost its position as the nation's top black-owned-and-operated record label. That status was now enjoyed by Columbia's Def Jam, headed by rap mogul Russell Simmons. Many of the other mainstream companies had also pulled in a considerable chunk of the black pop and urban contemporary markets. In addition, the soft-pop sound that had been Motown's trademark was now eclipsed by harder-edged forms of black music; gangsta rap and "new jack swing" (hip-hop rhythms mixed with R&B harmony) ruled the *Billboard* charts and radio airwaves. When they signed Boyz II Men, Motown also contracted with another male group managed by Bivins, a preteen sextet from Georgia named Another Bad Creation (ABC). Motown hoped that ABC, along with labelmates the Boyz and Shanice Wilson, a former winner on the popular "Star Search" televison program, would help Motown become the "Sound of Young America" again.

When Shanice Wilson's first single, a delightful pop ditty called "I Love Your Smile," went gold and reached number one on the R&B chart and number two on the pop chart at the beginning of 1991, Motown had its first top-five hit in six years. They were definitely back in the game.

Motown executives saw Boyz II Men as another potential winner, but there was disagreement about how to present them to the world. Instead of having the group dress like the current crop of male rap artists—in low-riding baggy pants, untied name-brand sneakers and boots, oversize T-shirts, and baseball caps—Bivins envisioned a middle-class look similar to that of Alex Vanderpool, a character on his favorite soap opera, *All My Children*. This wardrobe included loose chino pants, Bermuda shorts, Bally loafers, sports coats, bow ties, striped shirts, and block-patterned sweaters. He wanted the Boyz to be hip but also to follow in the footsteps of Motown stars such as the Temptations and the Four Tops, who were classy yet cool, well groomed and well mannered, slick and sexy.

Mike, however, thought that Bivins's outfits would make the Boyz look less like future recording sensations than not-with-it nerds. "Michael said, 'Nothing can match,'" Mike explained. "We tried it, but when we walked down Hollywood Boulevard, every car stopped and people just stared at us. We tried to stay cool but we felt like fools. Shawn would say, 'That's cool. It just means we're different.' But all I could think was, 'Yeah, we're different all right.'" Mike was not alone in feeling the way he did. "They [the people at Motown] did not say anything, they just smiled," he recalled. "But as soon as we left the room, they'd laugh about us behind our backs."

But Bivins knew the importance of the right image: he had learned the tools of the trade from one of the masters of the game, Maurice Starr. Starr had discovered Bivins, Ronnie DeVoe, Ricky Bell, Bobby Brown, and Ralph Tresvant when all five lived in the Roxbury Orchard Park projects in Boston. He named the talented vocal quintet New Edition and turned them into the 1980s version of the Jackson Five, thanks to sugarcoated soul cuts like "Candy Girl" and "Popcorn Love." After he opted out of managing New Edition, Starr did it all over again—but this time the five youngsters were white. By the late 1980s, Starr's New Kids on the Block were the reigning kings of soul-laced bubblegum pop. Having watched Starr in action, Bivins was packaging Boyz II Men with an eye to dazzling young women, who are the backbone of the record-buying public. His aim was to make the Boyz into teen heartthrobs like New Edition and New Kids on the Block.

Jackie Wilson, best known for hits such as "Lonely Teardrops" and "Higher and Higher," was one of the leading artists associated with Berry Gordy. Wilson was equally adept at romantic ballads and gospel-infused numbers; his stylistic versatility would later become a trademark of Boyz II Men.

This photo captures Boyz II Men in the casual dress their manager, Michael Bivins, rarely permitted them to wear onstage. By outfitting the Boyz in elegant outfits that recalled the singing groups of the 1950s, Bivins gave them a distinctive identity on the contemporary music scene.

Bivins also felt he was carrying on a time-honored tradition begun by Berry Gordy. Gordy had made a specialty of molding and shaping young men and women barely out of their teens into polished, poised artists, his greatest creation being the Supremes. Like the other Boyz, Mike eventually came to see Bivins's strategy as a smart one: "I guess the bottom line was that we had to not only sound different but look different. If we came out dressed like everybody else, we might not capture people's attention. We could get lost in the crowd. The sad fact is that, in this business, talent is not the only thing you need. You've got to have a gimmick, you've got to be able to show folks what sets you apart from everyone else. And I guess this was what we had to offer."

If Motown still had some doubts that Boyz II Men's fashion statement was the way to go, they were probably even more concerned when the Boyz wished to record their own material. The company allowed Shanice to do this, but she worked under the guidance of Narada Michael Walden, who was responsible for bringing number-one hits, as well as Grammy awards, to Whitney Houston ("I Wanna Dance With Somebody"), Aretha Franklin ("Freeway of Love"), and Mariah Carey ("Vision of Love"). The Motown executives did not have the same confidence in the head producer working with Boyz II Men: Dallas Austin was an 18-year-old Atlantan whose main claim to fame was producing a moderate hit for rappers Doug E. Fresh and Irby called "Mr. D.J." Austin also produced ABC, but their multiplatinum debut had not made its mark when the Boyz II Men project was being planned.

However, when Motown heard the finished product, recorded in six weeks at Philadelphia's Studio 4, all their fears vanished. The 10-song set featured 5 songs cowritten by the Boyz and 2 others by Nate alone. The Boyz also arranged all the lead and background vocals. The two sides of the album were aptly titled "Adagio" ("slow tempo" in Italian) and "Allegro" ("quick, lively"), no doubt a nod to their classical music background in high school. The first side consisted of smoky ballads, from the sweet yet sad "Please Do Not Go" to the sexy and sassier "Uhh Ahh." The second side showed that Boyz II Men could both work a love song and kick a serious groove. One tune was unabashedly autobiographical. "Motownphilly" recapped their story: growing up in the city, meeting each other, forming the group at the High School of the Creative and Performing Arts, hooking up with Bivins, and living their dream. At one point in the track, the music stops and the Boyz do an a cappella jazz break in the style of Take Six. The song would also announce the group's philosophy about their music: "Not too hard, not too soft."

There was only one tune on the album not composed specifically for or by Boyz II Men: "It's So

Boyz II Men sing a capella at Motown's 1990 Soul by the Sea concert in Montego Bay, Jamaica. Due to their exceptional musicianship and vocal skill, Boyz II Men can perform in any setting, with or without instrumental backing.

Hard to Say Goodbye to Yesterday," which was first performed by G. C. Cameron in the 1975 film *Cooley High*. The popular movie explored the friendship between a group of black teenagers during the 1960s, and it was obviously a favorite of the Boyz: they decided to call the finished album *Cooleyhighharmony*. Unlike the version of the song in the movie, the Boyz did their rendition a cappella, and on this tune their trademark vocal style can be fully appreciated.

As Wanya explained, "Shawn has a soft, sultry voice, the sound of a classically trained singer. Nate's voice has the R&B bottom and a pop-soul feel. I bring a stronger, gospel flavor with my voice, with runs and ad-libs. And Mike is the true bottom, the bass, the thing that links us. So together, we contain elements that can appeal to any kind of ear."

Motown obviously agreed: the voices of Boyz II Men were so rich and fluid that no electronic enhancing was needed, and the label decided to release the album "unmixed." At the time, this rarely happened in the pop music field. Years had passed since singers simply cut a track and let it stand as it was. For example, Roberta Flack's first album, *First Take* (1969), literally lived up to its title: all eight songs were done in one take, and the entire recording session took just 10 hours. Today, in the music video age, artists have been able to make up for the lack of a true singing voice by using technology in the studio to improve the sound of their vocals. But because Boyz II Men treated their voices as instruments and knew how to use them to create a sharp, clear sound, there was no need to meddle with their recordings.

Finally, the moment of truth had arrived. Motown hosted a party at the Capital Children's Museum in New York City, celebrating the debut albums of both Boyz II Men and ABC. Just weeks later the Boyz' first single would have its premiere on radio stations, and the album would hit record stores. Naturally, the young performers were nervous. "We enjoyed what we created and just prayed that what we did was loved by someone," recalled Wanya. He and the other Boyz had nothing to worry about.

5

The Beginning of the Road

THE YOUNG SINGERS vividly remembered the first time they heard themselves on the radio. "We all heard it together, but we were listening to it while driving in different cars," explained Mike. "It came on a Philly station called WDAS. Later, when I got home and called Nate, he said, 'Man, we almost had an accident over it!' We were all so excited, we practically did back flips."

They were not the only ones. The critics weighed in with their opinions, and the reviews were more than just good. "Their doo-wop hip-hop soul is revolutionary and right on time," said the *Washington Post*. *The Detroit Free Press* added, "Boyz II Men carry on the tradition of barber shop quartets and street corner crooners in a brilliant way." And New York's *Amsterdam News* declared, "*Cooleyhighharmony* is one of the best debuts from an act in years."

The big test, though, would be the public's response—and Boyz II Men passed with flying colors. Thanks to a fast-paced video in which the Boyz

Boyz II Men receive the 1992 Billboard *award, one of the many honors they accumulated after the success of their debut album,* Cooleyhighharmony.

wore their trademark Vanderpool gear and took viewers on a tour of their neighborhoods and the High School of the Creative and Performing Arts, "Motownphilly" shot to number one on *Billboard's* R&B chart and, several weeks later, made the pop music top five. The single's popularity helped push *Cooleyhighharmony* to the top spot on *Billboard's* R&B album chart and into the top 10 in the pop album rankings.

All in all, the reception of "Motownphilly" shocked the Boyz. "We did not think it would jump out as big as it did," explained Mike. "We wanted to drop a ballad first because that's how we see ourselves." Nate added, "While the song was definitely a reflection of who we were lyrically, it did not really represent us musically. We're more the relaxed, chill out type of guys. We love slow jams."

The Boyz felt more at home with "It's So Hard to Say Goodbye to Yesterday," which was released as their next single. It was, though, a risky move: in the technologically driven music industry, a cappella tunes get almost no radio airplay. And compared to "Motownphilly," the ballad was overtly sentimental; some believed it would be a weak follow-up to the first single. But "It's So Hard to Say Goodbye to Yesterday" immediately became the theme music for many high school proms and graduation ceremonies across the country. It also enabled Boyz II Men to attract another audience: the parents of their original fans. Many adults had grown up with the *Cooley High* version of the song, and they too rushed to record stores to buy Boyz II Men's rendition. The musical generation gap that had always separated the young from the old was bridged as the Boyz revived the old-school doo-wop of 1950s groups like the Platters, the Flamingos, and the Drifters.

"This was no small accomplishment," observed pop music critic Leonard Pitts, Jr. "We're talking

about elders who, by definition, hate the music their children listen to. Just the idea that your mother or father would like something you do, I'm sure, was weird to a lot of the kids. As far as they knew, the Boyz were doing something no one had ever done before. But their parents had heard it before—and they were probably shocked themselves to find out that the song had been brought back by young men who were the same age as their sons and daughters."

Sean Cort witnessed this reaction firsthand. As both a disc jockey and the program director on WRKS-FM, an R&B station in New York, he recalled the requests his station received to hear the song at the height of its popularity:

> We'd open up the phone lines and two out of every three people would be calling about it. At least half of them were over the age of 35 and had no problem

A scene from the 1975 film Cooley High. Boyz II Men *recaptured the popular film's aura in their debut album, which included a new rendition of* Cooley High's *theme song, "It's So Hard to Say Goodbye to Yesterday."*

testifying to that fact. They would say how they were in high school when Cooley High came out and danced many a dance to that song under blue lights. They said it took them back, to the good old days. There were even a few who admitted that, the first time they heard the Boyz' version, they cried. That's how powerful the song is. But it was also a testament to how talented the Boyz were.

As a result, the single became Boyz II Men's second number-one R&B hit and peaked at number two on the pop chart. Like "Motownphilly," it was certified platinum, meaning that one million copies had been sold. Moreover, with their first two singles, the Boyz had established themselves as a group that really could not be pigeonholed. "[With 'Motownphilly'], people assumed that we were just an R&B group that borrowed from new jack swing and rap," said Mike. "Then, we just let the voices do the speaking for us. We wanted to show people that they could never suspect what we were going to do."

Boyz II Men had certainly qualified for the show business label of "overnight sensation." They were everywhere: MTV and BET; the Apollo Theater and "Soul Train"; Hal Jackson's annual Talented Teens Contest and Lou Rawls's Parade of Stars Telethon, which raised funds for the United Negro College Fund.

Before long, they were reaping accolades as well. The National Association for the Advancement of Colored People (NAACP) gave Boyz II Men the organization's Image award for Best New Musical Artist of 1991. The Boyz received the same citation from both the American Music awards and the Soul Train Music awards, which also named "Motownphilly" the best R&B single. Though they missed out on the Grammy for Best New Artist, they picked up the Best Vocal by an R&B Group or Duo for *Cooleyhighharmony*.

Hammer, shown here at the 1990 MTV Music awards, was the hottest star in rap music when Boyz II Men joined his Too Legit to Quit tour as an opening act in 1992. Unlike many other rappers, Hammer did not glorify violence or put down women.

Perhaps the most gratifying prize for a musician is the admiration of fellow artists, and this was quick in coming. Fellow Motown star Stevie Wonder invited Boyz II Men to do background vocals on his sound track for Spike Lee's film *Jungle Fever*. Johnny Gill, another former member of New Edition, used not only the group's vocals but also their song-writing abilities; the Boyz wrote and performed on "I

Got You," which was featured on Gill's second Motown album, *Provocative*. In addition, the Boyz contributed "Sympin' Ain't Easy" to the sound track of *White Men Can't Jump*.

The greatest coup of all for Boyz II Men was being tapped as the opening act for MC Hammer's concert tour in April 1992. At that time, Hammer was the undisputed king of what one critic called "safe rap." Instead of downing women and glorifying violence like other rap artists, he praised God ("Pray") and congratulated himself on his own style ("U Can't Touch This"). The album featuring these two songs, *Please Hammer Don't Hurt 'Em*, sold a whopping 10 million copies in 1990 and brought Hammer three Grammys and a slew of American Music awards. He dropped the initials in front of his name when his third album, *Too Legit to Quit*, was released. (Ironically, when the Too Legit to Quit tour kicked off, Hammer's album sat some 10 places below *Cooleyhighharmony* on the pop chart.)

The Boyz would be sharing the duty of opening Hammer's show with another male quartet: two sets of brothers called Jodeci, whose sexually suggestive lyrics got them tagged the "Bad Boyz II Men." "Naturally, people just knew there was going to be some static between us but there was not," said Wanya. "We were two totally different groups that were not competing for the same ear, the same audience. Besides, we all respected what the other did. There is definitely room for all of us."

But just a month after Boyz II Men hit the road with Hammer and were given a quadruple platinum award (four million copies sold) for *Cooleyhighharmony* from Motown, tragedy struck. On Memorial Day, the Boyz' road manager, Khalil Rountree, was shot to death in an elevator at the Gold Coast Hotel in Chicago, where the Boyz and their troupe were staying. Rountree's assistant and childhood friend, Quadree El-Amin, was wounded during the

attack but survived. Apparently, two of the three assailants responsible for the attack worked at the hotel and had helped El-Amin take everyone's luggage up to the rooms earlier that day. They must have learned that Rountree was Boyz II Men's manager and, assuming that he had a large amount of cash to pay the musicians and other tour members, went to his room during the early hours of the morning with the intention of stealing the money. Their plan went awry when they found Rountree still awake. As Rountree and El-Amin were taking the men down to hotel security, one of them pulled a gun and opened fire.

The incident did not surprise some critics of the current music scene. A number of rap artists, as well as some R&B acts, had gotten a reputation for being

Boyz II Men's road manager, Khalil Rountree (center), also served as a mentor and father figure to the group. When Rountree was shot to death during an attempted robbery in Chicago, his loss deeply affected the four young artists. They later dedicated an album to Rountree, saluting his "perseverance to see '[his] kids' succeed."

a bit too boisterous, with fistfights and shootings occurring both in hotels and concert halls. Some concert arenas and theaters in major cities even refused to book rap acts, fearing that violence would break out.

Boyz II Men, however, lived up to their clean-cut, all-American image. And despite his six-foot, 250-pound frame, so did Rountree. As Michael Mitchell, senior vice president of communications for Motown, told the media, "Some rap, R&B and rock groups have seedy characters that hang around with them on the road, but Boyz II Men are not that kind of group. They are peaceful and so was Khalil."

The gunman was eventually convicted and sentenced to 14 years in prison, but Rountree's murder deeply affected Boyz II Men for a long time. That anyone they knew should be killed in such a senseless way would naturally have sickened and angered them. But Rountree was more than just an acquaintance or a business associate; he was a father figure to the group. A native of North Carolina who grew up in Newark, New Jersey, he began by promoting shows with classic R&B acts like the Manhattans and Blue Magic and then became a security guard and road manager for New Edition. He knew the ropes and schooled the Boyz in handling themselves on the road, surviving in the industry, and above all, truly growing from boys to men. Wanya explained Rountree's influence:

> I was from the projects; that's all I knew. I was *loud*. I did not know how to be polite. And I thought he [Rountree] could not stand me because of it. So I tried to better myself. But we had to do it for ourselves, not for him. We had to learn to be friends. So one day, he just told us off, said that we did not have any unity. I thought about it and he was right. It was not that we hated each other. It's just that we sang together better than we lived together. But if we expected to coexist, we had to keep things tight as a group, to be a real family to each other.

After they attended Rountree's funeral—where they sang "It's So Hard to Say Goodbye to Yesterday" with tears streaming down their faces—and took a week off to grieve, Boyz II Men resumed their spot in the tour. "We still had Khalil's murder lingering in our heads, but we also had a new sense of purpose," said Shawn. "Our loss somehow made us stronger. We did not continue working just to perform; we did it for Khalil. He worked very hard to get us to that point, and he would not have wanted our career to just crash and burn."

The whole tragic episode made the title of their next Boyz II Men single, released two months after Rountree's death, more than ironic: "End of the Road." But the record-breaking success of the song signaled the beginning of a new and even more prosperous road that the group was about to travel, with the spiritual guidance of Khalil Rountree.

6

A Stone Soul Christmas

THE *SEATTLE TIMES* went out on a limb and called "End of the Road" the "most emotionally charged single of the 1990s." The *Michigan Chronicle* stated that "Boyz II Men harmonize with passion and compassion we have not heard since the Spinners and Harold Melvin and the Bluenotes in the seventies." And Gladys Knight, who loved the song so much that she would record it two years after the Boyz, proudly proclaimed, "They found that magic that has been missing in so much of the music today."

All this praise for "End of the Road" was hardly overstated. The single became so hot that it put the Boyz at the top of the charts for a history-making 13 weeks. While the film it was taken from, *Boomerang*, made a quick exit from the nation's movie theaters, "End of the Road" became the song of the summer of 1992. It blared from radios in urban and suburban areas, on beaches, in parks and playgrounds, even at bars and clubs as the last dance of the night (or morning). It hypnotized the nation, bringing

Among the many honors reaped by Boyz II Men in 1993 was the Grammy award for Best R&B Vocal Group, their second in a row.

back romance in full effect, and it also had an effect on *Cooleyhighharmony*. Riding the crest of the wave, *Cooleyhighharmony* leaped back into the top 10 on the pop album chart (finding a home at number 3 for several weeks) and rebounded to number 1 on the R&B chart, selling an additional two million copies.

The Boyz then switched gears and made their acting debut in the ABC-TV special miniseries *The Jacksons: An American Dream*, which dramatized the story of Katherine and Joe Jackson, whose eight talented children would eventually change the face of pop music. The Boyz had rather interesting roles: playing bullies who push around the oldest Jackson brothers, Jackie and Tito, in their hometown of Gary, Indiana. "As fellas who were always on the other end of it, being teased and taunted by other kids for being different, it was easy to do, not to mention fun," observed Nate.

Boyz II Men also sang in the film, doing a cover of the Five Satins' 1956 classic "In the Still of the Night." They knew they were taking a bigger chance doing this song than they had taken with "It's So Hard to Say Goodbye to Yesterday," because "In the Still of the Night" is considered one of the best recordings ever done in the rock and roll era. "No one had ever tried to touch it before," said Nate. "But we like to do things that are on the edge, to rise to the challenge of doing a song and making it sound like Boyz II Men."

Boyz II Men's version was so smooth that Motown received many requests from radio programmers (and fans) to release the song as a single. They complied, and the record went platinum and peaked at number two on the pop chart. Interestingly, the single that kept the Boyz from reaching the top spot was Whitney Houston's "I Will Always Love You," from the sound track of *The Bodyguard*, in which she also starred. Houston's producer,

David Foster, had apparently paid careful attention to the success of Boyz II Men's "It's So Hard to Say Goodbye to Yesterday": Houston sang a cappella for the first 30 seconds of "I Will Always Love You," which stayed at the top of the chart for 14 weeks, breaking the Boyz' record.

But when 1993 dawned, Boyz II Men was not to be outdone by Houston or anyone else in racking up the honors. The Boyz won an NAACP award and their second consecutive Grammy for Best R&B Vocal Group; two American Music awards for Favorite Soul Group and Favorite Pop Single ("End of the Road"); and three Soul Train Music awards for Best R&B Group, R&B Song of the Year, and Best R&B Music Video ("End of the Road"). And to top everything off, *Billboard* magazine christened Boyz II Men the Best International Group of the Year.

Some of the most important awards came not from the music industry establishment but from down home. When the Boyz returned to Philadelphia to host a free concert organized by the radio station that had given them their first exposure four years earlier, they were presented with a plaque with an inscription that read: "Discovered backstage in 1989, Center Stage in 1993, Congratulations to Philadelphia's own Boyz II Men, Power 99FM, October 22, 1993." They also received an invitation to a "party" they could not refuse: President Bill Clinton's inaugural celebration in Washington, D.C.

"One of our best times on the road was at the White House," Mike told Rita Henderson. "When we walked through the White House, we saw many paintings of people whose names we did not always know, but we knew that they had been a part of United States history. The art work was simply incredible. President Clinton is one of the nicest people we ever met, and we like his progressive nature."

Eddie Murphy and Robin Givens starred in Boomerang, *a romantic comedy released in 1992. The movie quickly vanished from the nation's theaters, but Boyz II Men's performance of "End of the Road," a song from the sound track, became a record-breaking hit.*

The Five Satins' "In the Still of the Night" has endured as an R&B classic since its release in 1956. No other group had ever dared to record the song until Boyz II Men's 1993 cover version, a hit with both critics and record buyers. "We like to do things that are on the edge," said Shawn.

In addition to all of this, the Boyz found the time to perform on MTV's "Unplugged" series and on the station's own Inaugural Ball; the NBA Stay in School Jam; the Rock and Roll Hall of Fame awards; and the Britt Music awards in London. With all this activity, it was a miracle that they had room on their schedule to record their next album. In the wake of two mighty hit singles, the public responded enthusiastically to the news that Boyz II Men's sophomore effort would be out in November 1993. When it arrived, though, it was far different from anything people had been expecting.

Christmas Interpretations was both an unusual Christmas offering and an odd project for the Boyz to tackle. In the record industry, it was almost unheard of for a new artist to do a holiday album as a second effort. Though records of this type can enjoy a long shelf life, most barely sell 250,000 copies even if they have been in record stores for decades. There are only a handful of exceptions to this rule, one of them being Nat King Cole's *Christmas Song*, which sells between 30,000 and 50,000 copies every year.

But the Boyz were not deterred by these facts. "We *felt* this project," Shawn explained when asked why the group decided to do it. "We would not have been true to our craft if we did not listen to our inner voices telling us that this was what we had to do and now was the time to do it. Besides, *everybody* loves Christmas . . . and we wanted to express our views of Christmas, reflecting what it meant to us growing up and what it means to us now."

Instead of choosing Dallas Austin as their producer again, Boyz II Men now teamed up with Brian McKnight. McKnight's debut album on Mercury Records had spent over a year on *Billboard*'s R&B chart, while his duet with Vanessa Williams, "Love Is," culled from the sound track of the prime-time soap opera *Beverly Hills 90210*, was both a number-one adult contemporary (easy listening) and top-five pop hit. The match was a perfect one: McKnight's supple, syrupy singing and songwriting style fit the Boyz perfectly. "Brian understood that we wanted this album to be soft and very warm," said Shawn. "We wanted it to sound like Christmas but we also wanted it to be us."

To get the effect they wanted and to have the album stand out from the hundreds of other Christmas collections already on the market, Boyz II Men rejected the idea of doing a package of traditional Yuletide tunes, such as "Jingle Bells," "O Come, All Ye Faithful," or "Hark, the Herald Angels Sing." The only traditional song they chose was "Silent Night," which they did a cappella in two versions— one to open the set, the other to close. Sandwiched in between these performances were eight new compositions, all of them penned by the Boyz with the collaboration of McKnight. They believed that their approach would do something that most Christmas albums did not do. "We wanted our celebration of Christmas to be the kind just right for a quiet evening by the fire, snuggling up to that special someone as the snow falls outside," explained Nate. "We set out to capture that type of setting, that type of mood."

And that they did. While reminding listeners why the holiday is celebrated ("A Joyous Song," "Why Christmas," "Do They Know"), the album also explores the happiness that loved ones can bring during the holiday ("Share Love") and addresses the sadness that some people experience during the season ("You're Not Alone"). One track even recalls the surprise of falling in love on Christmas Day ("Who Would Have Thought").

When the reviews came in, there were no Scrooges among the nation's music critics. *Pulse*, the magazine published by the Tower Records chain, said that *Christmas Interpretations* "makes you

Three of the Boyz look over a script with Dick Clark, whose career as a music emcee dates back to the early days of rock and roll. By combining a 1990s vibe with timeless R&B harmonies, Boyz II Men's first two albums struck a chord not only with young listeners but also with older generations nostalgic for the past.

want to celebrate Christmas all year round. You will not only listen to it during December." The *Atlanta Tribune* echoed this sentiment, thanking the Boyz for "a spiritually uplifting, soulful smorgasbord." And *Entertainment Weekly* gave the album an A, its second-highest grade.

Christmas Interpretations sold one million copies in its first two months of release, becoming Motown's best-selling Christmas album ever (this time the Boyz conquered the Jackson Five) and one of the most successful seasonal projects ever recorded. The video for "Let It Snow," the only single culled from the album, no doubt helped boost sales. In the video, the Boyz and four female friends are shown in a log cabin blanketed by snow, exchanging gifts, kissing under the mistletoe, and gathering around a grand piano for caroling. The images are so genuine that they would be perfect for the cover of a Christmas card. "Let It Snow" did not exactly become another smash (it only reached the pop top 40), but it did garner Boyz II Men their third consecutive Grammy nomination for Best R&B Group.

The success of *Christmas Interpretations* made Boyz II Men an intimate part of many Christmas events. The mayor of New York, David Dinkins, invited the group to attend the traditional lighting of the city's giant Christmas tree in Rockefeller Center. They then performed the songs for an animated special called "A 'Cool Like That' Christmas," which featured the voices of actress Whoopi Goldberg and New York Knicks basketball star Patrick Ewing. Then the Boyz helped ring in 1994 on one of the traditional New Year's Eve TV specials. Boyz II Men even got to play Santa Claus at Hale House in Harlem, putting smiles on the faces of infants and children, some of them drug addicted and others infected with AIDS.

But once the glow of the holiday season faded, the Boyz knew that their fans would not be totally satisfied with a holiday album; the public was expecting *Cooleyhighharmony*, part two. So early in the year the group headed back into the studio to record another album. This one would not only solidify their title as the leaders of the male group harmony craze; it would also put them in the history books once again.

7

The Second Time Around

THE BOYZ KNEW that *Cooleyhighharmony* would be a tough act to follow. As anticipation and speculation about their next project began to grow, they became just as antsy and anxious as the public. "It was not the awards that made us nervous, but the sales," said Nate. "This industry makes you think you have to top yourself everytime. If you do not, they look at you as if you have failed, and you are forgotten."

Because of this, the new album—simply entitled *II*—took a lot more time to plan, prepare, and produce. While *Cooleyhighharmony* had been done in less than two months with a single producer, *II* was crafted and conceived over nine months in five different cities with 11 different producers, who included all the Boyz, either singly or together. Of the 30 songs originally recorded for the project, the Boyz chose 13.

According to Nate, it was a difficult but necessary process of elimination: "All the songs [we

After a multiplatinum debut album and a top-selling Christmas album, Boyz II Men felt enormous pressure to repeat their success as they prepared their next project, appropriately entitled II.

71

recorded] were great, but some just did not fit. When we record, we just do not put hits on an album, or a couple of hits and filler. [Doing an album] is like an art or a puzzle. Every song has a different purpose. We try to give it more legs to stand on. It's like a movie, and each song is a different scene."

The first half of *II* consists of up-tempo ("U Know" and "Thank You," a "funkdafied" prayer) and mid-tempo jams ("Vibin' It" and "I Sit Away"), on which new jack riffs and samples rule. The second half of the album is devoted, in Mike's words, to "maxin' and relaxin'." Here quiet storm ballads

Boyz II Men accepting Grammy awards for their third album, II. *The quartet spent nine months preparing and recording 30 songs for the album: out of this group, they chose the 13 cuts that fit together best. "It's like a movie, and each song is a different scene," explained Nate.*

abound, and the Boyz knew exactly where to look for them. Babyface contributed two selections ("Water Runs Dry" and "I'll Make Love to You"), while Jimmy Jam and Terry Lewis, best known for their work with Janet Jackson, provided *II* with "On Bended Knee."

As they did on *Cooleyhighharmony* and *Christmas Interpretations*, the Boyz wrote or cowrote most of *II*'s tracks, including "Khalil," a tribute to their late friend and road manager. They also dipped into their well of musical knowledge, merging the old with the new. While they deliver a crisp, gospel-inflected a cappella version of the Beatles classic

"Yesterday," they effortlessly fuse hip-hop and cabaret jazz on "Jezzebel."

Throughout *II*, the Boyz continued to share lead vocal duties, having learned an important lesson from their experience with former group member Marc Nelson. "No one person should dominate the group because we are a group, not a solo act," explained Shawn. "We give each other the chance to express ourselves through both writing and song. Groups break up because some members are pushed to the background while others are pushed or force themselves to the front. That is not going to happen with us."

The majority of the reviews for *II* were nothing less than fabulous. The *St. Louis Post-Dispatch* said, "*II* was worth the wait. . . . The Boyz have not only topped themselves, they've outdone themselves." *New York Newsday* praised the Boyz for what it called their "sophisticated soul" and said, "*II* is filled with such tasty tracks that it is almost good enough to eat." *Time* magazine stated that "Boyz II Men is living, singing proof that the love song—like love itself—will never really disappear."

However, a few critics complained that *II* was "less street" than *Cooleyhighharmony* and that the Boyz were watering down their sound to appeal to a more mainstream (white) audience. One commentator went so far as to label their style "bleached soul." But the Boyz balked at such a notion.

"The idea that, if you're black, you have to sound or sing a certain way is racist," argued Shawn. "Not everybody in the black community likes raunchy music or artists with a hard-core street image, just like not all white people like heavy metal music. We're accepted by people in the black community and the white community who like this kind of music because of what it says, not because of who is doing it. Music is for the people; it has no color."

Shawn also dismissed the belief that Boyz II Men were "downplaying their blackness": "That's just ridiculous. We're young black men who grew up in the hood and we're proud of it. And the fact that we are being accused of such things shows that color is all that some people want to see. Because of who you are, they want to fit you into a nice little neat box, based on their own stereotypes."

The song that inspired these charges was "I'll Make Love to You," the album's first single release. While just as emotionally charged as the Boyz' past work, it has more of a pop feel: it starts out low-key and builds to a dramatic climax, following the standard of a Whitney Houston ballad. And, despite its suggestive title, it is not as gritty as some of their other sensual tracks, like "Uhh Ahh."

Ironically, the Boyz had originally been reluctant to record "I'll Make Love to You." Though they loved the song, they believed it resembled their past hit "End of the Road" (also by Babyface) too much. "We did not want to repeat ourselves, and in a way we felt like we would be if we included it on the album," Mike stated.

But record buyers did not have the same doubts as the Boyz or their critics. "I'll Make Love to You" became the group's second number-one pop single, tying the record that Whitney Houston's "I Will Always Love You" set after it stayed at the top of the chart for 14 weeks in 1993. The president of Motown, Jheryl Busby, had a simple explanation for the song's popularity. "America right now is being bombarded with reality," Busby noted, "whether it's talk shows or rap or trials on TV or C-Span. This is a group that once again is introducing us to fantasy."

That "fantasy" is really a belief in a concept that artists who have chosen to embrace lust, violence, and sexism in their work seemed to have forgotten about. As *Time* magazine noted, in Boyz II Men's world "women aren't objects of lust; they are cherished. 'Girl, your wish is my command / I'll submit to your demands,' go the lyrics to *I'll Make Love II You*. Monogamy is celebrated. 'Wanna build a new life,' goes *On Bended Knee*. 'Gonna make you my wife / Raise a family.' Boyz II Men has found a niche by being blissfully unaware of its cultural surroundings."

"We sing about love," explained Shawn. "Finding [it], enjoying [it], dealing with not having [it]. You won't find us singing anything overly sexual." He gives credit for this approach to the women who have served as role models for all the Boyz—their mothers. "They were the only figures, most of our years anyway, the ones who taught us how to respect girls. My mom told me to open doors for girls and pull out their chairs. I never understood why until I started doing it and saw that it made them feel nice. Women go through a great deal, and we feel the man should be the one to say, 'Hey, relax, now I'm going to do the things you want to be done.' That's the message we are sending."

Both Nate and Wanya backed this up. "The way we would be with a woman is exactly the way we express it on the album," Nate said. "We don't go out and say, 'Okay, let me smack your booty and flip you,' and all that crap." Wanya summed up the Boyz' attitude in one telling sentence: "I couldn't see disrespecting a woman, then seeing someone disrespecting my mom."

Nate added that the Boyz' message reached men as well as women. "Girls buy our records because we do not call them names. And guys who buy our records say they got it for their girls, but I think a lot of them want to be able to say the things we say, but they can't." There was concrete evidence to support his theory: "I can't tell you how many brothers who are hard-rocks, you know, really street, that come up to me, to us, and say that they love our music."

Boyz II Men's ability to attract such a variety of fans was a testament not only to their talent but also to their staying power. In the two years that separated the advent of *Cooleyhighharmony* and the release of *II*, over a dozen new male vocal groups had hit the scene, including Portrait, H-Town, Silk, and Shai. A number had attained a degree of success—Shai's single "If I Ever Fall in Love" reached number two on the pop charts and went gold, and Silk's "Freak Me" was a number-one pop hit for six weeks. But none could touch *Cooleyhighharmony*.

The Boyz were not comfortable being viewed as the ambassadors of this male vocal renaissance.

Accompanied by Michael Bivins and Motown president Jheryl Busby (standing, right), Boyz II Men display some of their platinum and gold records during an appearance at New York's Hard Rock Café.

"The only reason people might look on us as leaders is because we were among the first ones," admitted Wanya. "There are so many good vocal groups out there that, had any of them come forward before we hit, it might have been their success paving the way for us. [All] we're doing is just carrying on the torch of the older singers. It's just a cycle that's going around."

The Boyz might have set a new chart record with "I'll Make Love to You" if they had not replaced themselves at number one. When "On Bended Knee" bumped "I'll Make Love to You" out of the top spot, the Boyz accomplished something that only the Beatles and Elvis Presley had done. Both singles went platinum, making Boyz II Men the only R&B act (as of early 1995) to have five singles sell over one million copies in the 1990s.

II made some chart and sales history of its own. A week after it hit record stores in September, the album debuted on the pop chart in first place, becoming only the second Motown album to achieve this feat (Stevie Wonder's *Songs in the Key of Life* was the first, in 1976). *II* went on to sell nearly four million copies in four months, making it one of Motown's fastest-selling titles ever.

To no one's surprise, *II* put the Boyz back in the winner's circle on the awards circuit. They received their third Soul Train Music award and second NAACP Image award for Best R&B Group; racked up three American Music awards for Favorite Pop Single, Pop Group, and Soul/R&B Group; and earned two Grammys, Best R&B Group (their third) and the newly instituted R&B Album of the Year.

The honor that meant the most to Boyz II Men, though, was their Grammy nomination for Record of the Year. Even though "I'll Make Love to You" lost to Sheryl Crow's "All I Wanna Do," the Boyz were thrilled to have been considered for the industry's highest honor. For the Boyz to be placed on a par with veterans such as Bonnie Raitt ("Love Sneakin' Up on You") and Bruce Springsteen ("Streets of Philadelphia") told the entire world that the group had really arrived. "To know that your peers respect you that much that they would acknowledge you [that way] was truly special to us," said Nate. "It was a sign that we're not just viewed as a group that is on the cover of all those teen magazines, that we're just not a singing group; we're also musicians. We're taken seriously as artists. All the hard work, all the sacrifice had paid off."

8

From Boys to Men

IN FOUR SHORT years, Boyz II Men had become the world's best-selling vocal group, achieving a level of international success that only a handful of artists accomplish in every generation. Because they are so young and impressionable, no one would have been surprised if their egos swelled with their record sales, making them difficult, if not impossible, to work with and live with. However, those who have watched Shawn Stockman, Mike McCary, and Nate and Wanya Morris evolve into musical superstars say they have not changed at all.

"They have not been spoiled yet," explained their former principal, Ellen Savitz. "They have the drive, the knowledge and confidence, and they're willing to do whatever it takes to make it, yet they are unassuming as can be. They never lose their centeredness, they know exactly who they are." Nate explained the group's ability to remain on an even keel: "When you've come from a background like we have, you know you can't take anything for

Boyz II Men arrive in Los Angeles in January 1995 to attend the American Music awards ceremonies. When the awards were handed out, the Boyz were honored for their latest hit single, "I'll Make Love to You."

granted. We're just so blessed to be doing what we've always wanted to do and know that, as quickly as everything has happened to us, it can just be over in the blink of an eye."

Religion is the rock on which all the Boyz base their careers and their lives. Viewers who have seen them accept an award on television know that they thank God before anyone else in their lives. Perhaps some people believe they are just going through the motions, but all four singers say they have come to fully understand how God has worked on them and with them. "We do not scratch our heads all the time now, thinking it is all a dream and we're gonna wake up," Nate explained. "It is in a way too good to be true but we know that it is not about us. That power to captivate thousands of people on stage or millions when a song is on the radio—no human has that kind of power. That's God talking through us. We just have to be positive with that power."

Even through the perspective of faith, the intensity of the public's enthusiasm still overwhelms the four young men at times. Some of their most vivid memories stem from their first headline tour at the beginning of 1995. Wanya recalled some of the wild events of that tour:

> Once we were in Texas and Nate wanted a longhorn hat. It was difficult to find, but after practically looking all over Texas, he found one. When we were leaving the concert, Nate was wearing it and we were entering our van while walking through a crowd of fans, when suddenly this girl grabbed and kept Nate's hat. She went around the side of the van and banged on the window yelling, 'I've got your hat!' At first Nate was a little upset; I mean, he loved that hat. But then he realized how happy having his hat made one of his fans, and then losing it did not bother him anymore.

On another occasion, the fans' desire for souvenirs almost went too far, as Wanya related:

One time while we were performing, Mike walked toward the edge of the stage and leaned over to sing to the audience. The girls in the front rows were very excited and, suddenly, one of them pulled him down into the audience by his necktie! It was a five foot drop. She must not have realized what she was really doing because she almost choked him. We were frightened. He was rescued, though, by some security guards. That told us to be careful about getting so close to the fans on the stage. One moment you're singing to them and before you know it, you're sitting in their laps! But you have to take it all in stride. It just comes along with the territory.

The Boyz do not have to worry about excessive admiration from their families, who, while happy with the way things have developed, still know the Boyz as "Bass" (Mike), "Squirt" (Wanya), "Slim"

Boyz II Men rehearse at the Shrine Auditorium in Los Angeles for their performance at the 1995 Grammy awards. At this point in their career, the quartet had become the world's best-selling vocal group.

(Shawn), and "Nate." "Our families keep us in check and make sure we do not get big heads," said Shawn. "Nothing's changed at home, because Mom is still Mom and Dad is still Dad. I mean, we come off a leg of the tour, we walk in the door with our Grammy and American Music Awards, they say how proud they are of us, but then they go, 'O.K., now do your homework or clean your room or pick up after yourself or do the dishes.'"

In fact, from the Boyz' perspective, only some of the people around them have changed, particularly more distant relatives and old acquaintances who suddenly believe themselves close friends. "They say money does strange things to people, but it is often the people who want a piece of the pie who trip," said Shawn. He continued:

> It's a shame when I see some of my classmates today who thought I was a nerd and called me bad names back then trying to get next to me. They now speak kindly and give me hugs, when they know full well that while we were in school, they were not one iota of my friend. I hate flattery when it's fake. And, there are folks who have been close to me for years that just do not get it. They are like, 'Oh, yeah, y'all are livin' large now,' but we have to remind them that we did not work just to live some lavish lifestyle, or to throw a couple of thousand dollars their way just because they are our friends or family members and we can give it to them.

Nate concurred: "Most people do not understand what it took and still takes to make Boyz II Men the group it is. It's true what they say: 'Money does not grow on trees.'"

Because money is not Boyz II Men's reason for singing, they are able to focus on their music rather than their superstar status. "They have a clear idea of what they can and can not expect of the industry," offered producer Jimmy Jam. "They know that you can't take all the glamour, your name up in lights seriously. This is a business, it's cutthroat, and it'll chew you up and spit you out. That's why so many other artists get burned, are spiritually destroyed by the industry. I can't see that happening [to the Boyz] because they are so stable."

They have also been wise enough to recognize good advice when they hear it. Mike recalled that when the Boyz were taping an episode of *The Arsenio Hall Show*, they had a chance to meet two original members of the Temptations, Otis Williams and Melvin Franklin: "They said do not worry about competition, 'cause there's always going to be competition. They said for us not to break up—whatever problems you have, sit down and talk them out. And they said to always keep it four—do not take one away, do not add one, so that it messes up the flow or the family spirit. We live by their words

Boyz II Men pose for photographers in March 1995 after adding the Soul Train Music award to their trophy case. Whenever they accept an award, the singers always begin their remarks by thanking God. "We're just so blessed to be doing what we've always wanted to do," says Nate.

because they have lived it and know. You could never buy insight like that."

And they expect that wisdom to carry them even further. Boyz II Men have numerous plans for the future, such as starting their own line of apparel and writing and producing for more of their friends. And of course there are the future Boyz II Men recordings, some of which may take them into other areas, such as country music. Boyz II Men renegotiated their contract with Motown in 1993; the new arrangement calls for the group to produce seven albums, guaranteeing them an estimated $20 to $30 million.

The contract marked a major commitment for Motown, but subsequent events clearly showed that Boyz II Men were not going to be a passing fad. In 1995, they appeared on *Forbes* magazine's annual list of the 40 highest-paid entertainers, and at a lavish concert at New York's Madison Square Garden, the group demonstrated that they were just beginning to reach their prime. Though the lineup included such popular performers as Montel Jordan, Mary J. Blige, and TLC, the *New York Times* reported that "Boyz II Men were the stars and the reason the audience had come and stayed, even waiting through painfully long set changes." Calling the group "gentlemen lovers for the 90's," the *Times* noted that they had "spent money on choreography and staging, and with their clean and romantic sexuality, they slayed the girls in the audience." The *New York Daily News* added, "The multi-, multi-titanium crooners pulled out every R&B schtick known to man and not only made it all work, but also made it cool."

No matter what comes their way, the four young Philadelphians feel that they are ready for it. "When Boyz II Men make music, when we perform, we just want to be the best we possibly can be . . . and go to new heights," Mike said. "We're just gonna take our time with it all. We just put God first in everything we have to deal with, so we do not have to worry about the outcome."

There is one tantalizing question they still have to answer: now that they are grown men, will they continue to call themselves "boyz"?

"We don't and will not ever see it as a contradiction," said Nate. "People might think, 'You can't keep a name like that forever. How will that sound, you're celebrating twenty years in the business and you're still the Boyz?' But Boyz II Men is a process. We've grown up in the group and we continue to grow. The more you learn, the closer you get to being a man, but you still retain some of that boyishness. The name means learning, and that will continue to happen everyday of our lives."

Albums

Cooleyhighharmony (1991)
Christmas Interpretations (1993)
II (1994)

Singles

"Motown Philly" (1991)
"Uhh Ahh" (1991)
"It's So Hard to Say Goodbye to Yesterday" (1991)
"End of the Road" (1992)
"In the Still of the Night (I'll Remember)"(1992)
"Let It Snow" (1993)
"I'll Make Love to You" (1994)
"On Bended Knee" (1994)

CHRONOLOGY

1971   Nathan Morris born on June 18 in Philadelphia; Michael McCary born on December 16 in Philadelphia

1972   Shawn Stockman born on September 26 in Philadelphia

1973   Wanya Morris born on July 29 in Philadelphia

1988   Nate, Mike, Shawn, and Wanya meet at Philadelphia High School of the Creative and Performing Arts; form singing group that briefly includes a fifth member, Marc Nelson

1989   Aspiring singers obtain impromptu audition with Michael Bivins, who agrees to become their manager and names them Boyz II Men

1990   Nate and Mike graduate from Performing Arts

1991   Shawn graduates from Performing Arts; Wanya graduates from Willingboro High School; Boyz II Men sign recording contract with Motown Records; record first album, *Cooleyhighharmony*; release three hit singles; appear on Lou Rawls Parade of Stars telethon

1992   Boyz II Men win Grammy Award for Best R&B Vocal Performance by a Duo or Group; single "End of the Road" remains at number one on the pop music chart for a record-breaking 13 weeks; Boyz II Men perform as opening act on MC Hammer's Too Legit to Quit tour; make acting debut in TV movie *The Jacksons: An American Dream*; sales of *Cooleyhighharmony* top five million

1993   Boyz II Men win NAACP Image award; attend inaugural celebration for President Bill Clinton; win second Grammy award; cited by *Billboard* magazine as Best International Group of the Year; release *Christmas Interpretations* album

1994   Boyz II Men release *II* with one million advance orders placed before album is shipped to stores; *II* spends 10 weeks at the top of the charts; Boyz II Men undertake worldwide tour; "I'll Make Love to You" spends record 14 weeks at top of singles chart and is replaced by "On Bended Knee"

1995   Boyz II Men embark on extensive U.S. tour

Boyette, Michael, with Randi Boyette. *"Let It Burn!": The Philadelphia Tragedy.* Chicago: Contemporary Books, 1989.

Ershkowitz, Miriam, and Joseph Zikmund II, eds. *Black Politics in Philadelphia.* New York: Basic Books, 1973.

Farley, Christopher John. "No Grunge, No Gangstas." *Time,* September 5, 1994.

Gillett, Charlie. *The Sound of the City: The Rise of Rock and Roll.* Rev. ed. London: Souvenir Press, 1983.

Gordy, Berry. *To Be Loved.* New York: Warner, 1995.

Hajari, Nisid, and Heather Keets. "Revenge of the Nerds." *Entertainment Weekly,* September 16, 1994.

Henderson, Rita Elizabeth. *The Boyz II Men Success Story: Defying the Odds.* Los Angeles: Aynderson Press, 1995.

Klots, Steve. *Richard Allen.* New York: Chelsea House, 1991.

"Most Loved Music Makers." *Teen,* March 1993.

Platt, Larry. "Boyz II Men in a Hurry." *Philadelphia Magazine,* August 1992.

Reynolds, J. R., and Craig Rosen. "Boyz II Men: The Triumph of a New Motown Sound." *Billboard,* September 17, 1994.

INDEX

INDEX

PICTURE CREDITS

JAMES EARL HARDY is a freelance feature writer and music critic whose byline has appeared in the *Atlanta Tribune, Essence, Emerge, Vibe, Newsweek, Entertainment Weekly*, the *Washington Post*, and the *Village Voice*. He is also a contributing writer for *YSB* (Young Sisters and Brothers), a magazine for African-American youth. His work has won the E. Y. Harburg Foundation Arts Writing Award and the American Association of Sunday and Feature Editors Grant, a Columbia Scholastic Press Feature Writing Citation, and two Educational Press Association Writing awards. He is an honors graduate of both St. John's University and the Columbia University Graduate School of Journalism. Hardy's first novel, *B-Boy Blues* (Alyson Publications), became a national best-seller after its publication in November 1994 and was nominated for a Lambda Literary Award for Best Title from a Lesbian and Gay Small Press.